# Homeless Children

Look for these and other books in the Lucent
Overview series:

# Homeless Children

## by Eleanor H. Ayer

LUCENT
BOOKS

LUCENT *Overview Series*

**Library of Congress Cataloging-in-Publication Data**

Ayer, Eleanor H.
    Homeless children / by Eleanor H. Ayer
       p.  cm. — (Lucent Books overview series)
    Includes bibliographical references and index.
    Summary: Discusses why children become homeless in the
United States, how they live, and what can be done to help them.
    ISBN 1-56006-177-4 (alk. paper)
    1. Homeless children—United States—Juvenile literature.
[1. Homeless persons. 2. Homelessness.]  I. Title.  II. Series.
HV4505.A93   1997
362.7'08'942—dc20                            96–17343
                                                         CIP
                                                         AC

Copyright © 1997 by Lucent Books, Inc.
P.O. Box 289011, San Diego, CA 92198-9011
Printed in the U.S.A.

# Contents

# Introduction

A home would be a place where me and my brothers and my mom could all sit down and eat supper together. There would be plenty of food and milk for all of us. After supper we would watch TV together or maybe play ball if we had a yard. Then we'd go to sleep, just our family, each person in their own bed. There wouldn't be no screaming or fighting, so I wouldn't be scared. And there wouldn't be trash everywhere.

THIS IS TWELVE-YEAR-OLD Fernando's* idea of a home, something he hasn't had for nearly two years. Fernando is homeless, but this does not mean he has no place to sleep. It means he has no *permanent* place to sleep. One night he slept in a shelter the city of New York provides for homeless people. Before that, he and his mother and brothers lived in a welfare hotel on the other side of town. They'd gone to the welfare hotel when they were evicted, forced to move, from his aunt's apartment in New Jersey. The landlord had told his aunt that her relatives had to leave or she would lose her apartment. They were living with his aunt in the first place because Fernando's father had lost his job and left home. When his mother could no longer pay the apartment rent alone, Fernando and his family became homeless.

Still, Fernando counts himself lucky. He's always had an inside place to sleep. On the street he's seen homeless people sleeping on park benches or over steam grates on the sidewalks, covering themselves with pieces of card-

*Names of certain people and places have been changed to protect the privacy of those whose stories are told in this book.

board. Those people have absolutely no place to go. At least Fernando has had a roof over his head each night. But he is very tired of shelter life, never knowing week to week where his next "home" will be.

## Is homelessness new?

It has been said that "the poor are always with us." Always, there have been Americans who had no permanent place to live. In the 1800s, homeless people went to almshouses, "alms" meaning charity that is given to the poor. Many of the children housed there were forced to work long hours under dangerous conditions in sweat-

*A homeless family poses for a photograph inside a shelter. Financial difficulties sometimes force families to leave their homes and take refuge in shelters, welfare hotels, and on the streets.*

shops or factories. Often they did not have enough to eat and rarely could they go to school. In the mid-1800s, social reformer Jane Addams started Hull House in Chicago, the first of many so-called settlement houses where poor people could find food, medical care, and a place to stay. Hull House's success led to the opening of settlement houses in many cities, with nurseries where babies could stay while their mothers worked and after-school programs for children. The settlement houses helped people learn to read and encouraged students to go to school.

## Homelessness throughout history

In the late 1800s and early 1900s, millions of immigrants came to the United States seeking a better life. Often several families lived together in one crowded tenement. Even the youngest children worked often for pennies a day. Back then the only help for the poor came from concerned individuals, churches, private organizations, or local communities. Many towns had "poor houses" where those in need could live, and an "overseer of the poor" to administer those services. Most people considered it a disgrace to be "on the town" or "in the poor house" and tried desperately to avoid that status.

In the 1930s, the United States went through the Great Depression. Across the country, thousands of people—many of them wealthy—lost their jobs, their life savings, and their homes. During the depression, the state and federal governments set up social service programs to help the poor. These programs have grown steadily larger until today the government is primarily responsible for taking care of poor and homeless people.

Homelessness may not be new, but the problem has gotten much worse in

*Social reformer Jane Addams improved the status of Chicago's poor during the mid-1800s by establishing Hull House, which offered shelter and services to the needy.*

*Thousands of Americans lost their homes and savings during the Great Depression. Many of the social service programs enacted by the government to help care for poor and homeless people during this difficult period remain in effect today.*

recent years. It is impossible to say precisely how many Americans are homeless because there is no single accepted way of counting them. The National Alliance to End Homelessness estimates that 750,000 Americans are homeless on any particular night, and that during a one-year period, between 1.3 and 2 million people will be homeless. This figure does not include people who are living temporarily with friends or family. The General Accounting Office in Washington, D.C., estimates that the number of homeless increases about 25 percent each year. Nearly one-third are families with children. Roughly 4 percent are youths living on their own.

Homelessness is a condition very difficult to reverse. Few remain homeless for just a few nights. The average length of time families stay in an emergency shelter is thirteen months. When they leave, it's rarely to go to a permanent home. More often they move in with relatives or land in government-supported housing.

Fifty years ago, homeless people were in a class by themselves, different from most Americans. Often they were elderly people or single men, hobos and tramps, who begged in the streets and slept in the alleys. Vagrants, as

*Homeless men of the early 1900s sit in their makeshift shelter under a bridge. Homeless people of that era mostly stayed out of sight of the general public.*

they were then called, were looked down upon by the rest of society. Their clothes were ragged, their teeth were rotten, they lived off charity and stayed out of sight of mainstream America.

Today that is not so. Homeless people of the 1990s often look no different from other Americans. Newsman Tom Brokaw concluded, after interviewing people in rural Iowa for an NBC special, "The homeless are people you know." Before they became homeless, many were middle-class families who lived in good neighborhoods, had steady jobs, and drove nice cars. Their children went to good schools, played on sports teams, wore nice clothes, and lived like other kids. But unlike most, these people got down on their luck, ran out of money, and lost their homes and belongings.

Homeless families are generally young and headed by a single parent, usually the mother. Her age is about twenty-seven, and typically she has two or three children whose average age is six. Greater percentages of black and Hispanic families are homeless than are Anglos or Asians.

## Children who have no choice

It is often assumed that people are homeless because they want to be, because they prefer this lifestyle. Some say the homeless are lazy, that if they worked harder to better their lives they wouldn't be homeless. But rarely are these claims true. They certainly are not true of homeless children, who have no control over where they live or how they feed themselves. Today 15 percent of homeless people are under age nineteen. Child poverty, says teacher and writer Jonathan Kozol, has increased 50 percent since the late 1960s. A third of all children belong to families whose income is below the poverty line. This does not mean that all of them are homeless, but the chances of their becoming homeless are far greater than for children not living in poverty.

Some children are even homeless at birth, born to drug- or alcohol-addicted mothers who have no home themselves. The state often claims these babies and supports them in hospitals or other institutions until a home can be found. But often finding a place can take so long that the children become known as "boarder babies." They may stay in a hospital long after they are able to walk, and have to be chained to their cribs so they don't wander away. Though homes may eventually be found for them, the children may suffer permanent damage from having lived since birth in an institution with limited love and personal care. Many will go through life with severe mental and emotional problems.

A large proportion of homeless children are teenagers, either runaways or "throwaways," kids whose parents want nothing to do with them. Many have left home to escape abuse and violence. Nearly half of all homeless children in New York City are teenagers. This estimate is probably true for the rest of the country, but can't be stated with certainty because homeless teens stay in the shadows and live on the streets. They hope they will not be noticed, for, as minors, they risk being turned over to government agencies, sent back to an abusive parent, or put into foster care.

## Growing up homeless

In pictures drawn by homeless children, writer Robert Coles has noticed, "the eyes are tiny, the ears lacking, the mouth a mere line, the bodies quite small. In these drawings, there is no sky, no sun. Nor is there ground. . . . These people are suspended in air." Indeed, being homeless is like floating in air. Homeless children and their families are wanderers; they have no roots. They're always waiting until a place can be found where they can unpack, where they can sit down in their own space and have some privacy.

So many comforts that people with homes take for granted are luxuries to homeless children. Walls are one such luxury. When a person has lived night after night in a barracks-style shelter, in one big gymnasium-size room with dozens of other families, having a room with walls and a door that can be closed is a wonderful thing.

A stove and refrigerator are also luxuries. "Folks say homeless people could save a lot of money if they didn't eat out all the time," says one girl who lives in an old station wagon with her family. "But there ain't no place to cook. We got no way to keep stuff cold or heat it up for meals. You can't cook when you're living in a car."

Homeless children dream of a safe, clean bed. When a person is used to sleeping in a quiet place, it's hard to imagine screaming, swearing, fighting, and gunfire going on all night long. Fourteen-year-old Doreen describes the room in which she and her family stayed for a short time: "There was a hole in the wall big enough for a person to walk through. There was blood on the sheets, and bugs on the soap."

Even going to school is a privilege for many homeless children, because moving from shelter to shelter means changing schools often. So much moving makes it difficult to study and to stay at grade level. And because they never live long in one place, it's tough to make friends. Homeless children often feel rejected and unwelcome at school.

*A homeless family tries to make ends meet by living out of their van while searching for work. Homeless children live without luxuries and without basic comforts such as stoves, refrigerators, and beds.*

Feelings of fear, insecurity, low self-esteem, and other psychological problems are some of the prices children pay for having no permanent place to live. Many become so depressed they talk about committing suicide. Others wet the bed, even when they get older. Some develop strange habits like pulling out their hair or teeth. Young children may regress—go backward—into infancy by talking baby talk or crawling after they can walk. Because events in their lives are rarely positive, homeless kids de-

*Most young people find life on the streets to be dismal and frightening. Feelings of hopelessness can cause homeless kids to have behavior problems in school or turn to crime.*

velop a negative attitude about the world. They feel that no one cares about them and that most people are out to take advantage of them.

Homeless kids grow up with many disadvantages. They may experience frustration and anger over the lack of a stable home and the inability to do anything about it. They may "act out" or be disruptive to call attention to their situation in the hope that someone will help. Some homeless kids may have behavior problems in school. Others may commit petty crimes and be sent to juvenile detention centers. As they get older, their misbehavior may become more serious, and many reach adulthood already carrying a criminal record.

Their schooling often interrupted, homeless kids fall behind academically, and large numbers drop out before finishing high school. Without a good education, they are unable to find work. Many turn to illegal ways of getting what they need and want. Also, lack of good food and health care in childhood can lead to severe health problems as adults, which prevents people from working even if they do have skills. Without jobs, they are destined to become homeless adults who end up raising homeless children, and so the cycle repeats itself one more tragic time.

# 1

# How Do Children Become Homeless?

When my father left my mother, he stopped supporting us and we had to go on welfare. After that, the landlady wouldn't take our rent check anymore. . . . She started harassing us. . . . We came home late one day from the park, and we saw the big yellow sign "Evicted" and the marshal was there. I got upset and I started crying.

POVERTY, FAMILY DISPUTES, unemployment, eviction, violence, and a lack of affordable housing all contribute to homelessness. Maria's family became homeless through eviction, one of the most common causes of homelessness. Usually people are evicted because they cannot pay the rent, but there can be other reasons. Sometimes their building is condemned. When a landlord doesn't make repairs, the building may become so run-down that the city orders it demolished. Fire may destroy it, leaving families with no place to go. Twelve-year-old Tara and her family moved into her grandmother's apartment when their home burned. But after several months, the landlord realized they weren't just visiting. He told Tara's grandmother that they had to leave or she would be evicted. The grandmother didn't want to force her family away, but she had no choice.

Family violence can also lead to homelessness. Nicole's family once lived in a nice duplex in a quiet neighborhood. But her parents argued a lot and Nicole's dad hit her mom. When he started abusing the children, Nicole's mom decided to leave. She and the children went

**"You don't walk up five flights *to* our apartment anymore. Since we've been evicted, five flights *is* our apartment.**

to a women's shelter to get help. It was the beginning of a cycle of homelessness.

Outside violence can also force a family to leave home. Parents decide to move so their children won't be exposed to shootings, drug dealing, and other crimes. But often they find no better place to go. Fifteen-year-old Elizabeth knows how it feels to leave for nowhere:

> Where we used to live . . . was really dangerous. The roof was very close, and we used to see people up there shooting guns or fighting. One morning, somebody was dead outside. I was really scared. . . . We used to be scared all the time, so my mother took us to the shelter.

Sometimes children become homeless even though their parents remain in the home. Kids who are abused or neglected and children with parents who have severe drug, alcohol, or criminal problems can be removed from their homes to keep them safe. Social workers investigate reports of child neglect, abuse, or similar problems, and if they find the children are in danger, they can remove them.

## Taking a child out of the home

In 1980 Congress passed the Child Welfare Act, which says that children may not be taken from their homes unless the danger to them is extreme. This law has good and bad points. Child psychologists and social workers say children should stay with one or both of their birth parents if at all possible. The trauma of removing a child from familiar surroundings, no matter how bad the situation is, can be very damaging. Nowadays when there are problems at home, social workers try to work with the parent or parents so the family can stay together. But when the abuse and neglect are so severe that the children are in danger, the social worker recommends removing them.

When a child is taken from a home, the parent or parents are usually ordered to attend a treatment program to help them overcome their problems. When they have changed, or become rehabilitated, the children may return home. But sadly, one out of every three children who does return home is later abused or neglected again—and some are even killed. The 1980 law was passed to keep families together, in hopes of helping children. But attempts to keep families together do not always benefit children.

Children who are removed from their homes may be taken to a group home or to a shelter, until a safer, more permanent home can be found. Shelters are supposed to be temporary and safe, but often they are little better than the parents' homes from which the children were taken.

Group homes are a long-term alternative to the overcrowded foster care system, but many of these homes are rough, dirty, and violent. When Shaundese was fifteen, she was sent to a teen center in downtown Brooklyn because her mother had discovered she was selling drugs.

> I could hardly sleep the first night I was there. The girls were nasty, and the mattresses were filthy. The whole place was unsanitary. Nobody searches you when you come in, so people bring in guns, knives, crack and weed. The girls try to impress you by sticking a gun to your head if you give them any trouble.

Some children become homeless simply because a parent is too young to care for them. Unmarried teenage mothers are those most likely to turn over their children to the state. These mothers have chosen not to put up their children for adoption, but they know they cannot care for them until their own lives are more stable. When a child becomes a "ward," under the protection of the state, he or she is placed in temporary care until the mother is ready to assume responsibility. Sometimes, when their lives are

*Most children who are wards of the state have teenage mothers who cannot care for them. These homeless children are placed in foster care until their parents are able to support them.*

better organized, these mothers do return to claim their children. But all too often kids who become wards of the state remain in foster care indefinitely.

It's not always a parent's inability to provide good care that causes a child to be removed from the home. Young people who repeatedly get into trouble or break the law may be placed in juvenile correction centers or group homes. Teenage runaways or throwaways may also be sent to these facilities. Young people who live on their own without adult supervision are known as "status offenders." Even though they have committed no crime, the fact that they are living on their own makes them a higher risk for criminal behavior.

## Placing a child in foster care

When children are removed from their homes, regardless of the reason, they often are sent to foster care. Today more than five hundred thousand American children are in

*A young man sits alone in a juvenile detention center. State-operated centers house runaways, throwaways, and young people who repeatedly break the law.*

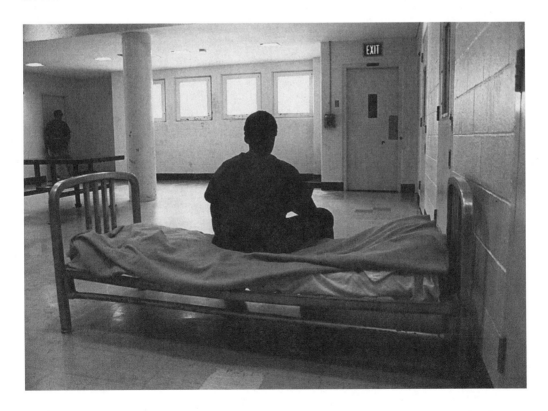

foster care and the number grows constantly. Only about 70 percent of those children actually live in foster homes; the rest are in temporary facilities waiting to be placed with families. But foster families are poorly paid, and unfortunately there are far fewer willing families than there are kids in need. Often the home is crowded or the "temporary" arrangement stretches into many months.

Foster families are screened to be certain that their homes are safe and caring places for children with problems. When adults are chosen to become foster parents, they attend training sessions where they learn about the problems and needs of the children who will come to them.

Children often arrive at a foster home dirty, underfed, and suffering from health problems. The new parents must care for those needs first. When the child is clean and healthy, foster parents can begin to treat the mind, heart, and soul, whose complicated needs require much more time and patience than providing clean clothes and warm food. Longtime foster care parents say a sense of humor is a must, along with lots of patience. In fact, the entire foster family must have a great deal of understanding. Foster children often have little respect for themselves or other people. It's important that the new family try not to place blame or accuse them of wrongdoing. If the foster child demands constant attention (as many abused children do), parents must gently but firmly balance the child's needs against all other responsibilities. Most important, the foster family should treat the child as a member of the household, being careful never to make him or her feel like an outsider.

But even when a foster family is good and kind, life for a foster child can be very difficult. Eleven-year-old Kenneth has lived with his foster family for two months:

> It's nice here. Everyone treats me fair, and I have my own bicycle. My foster brother and sister are good to me, but the kids at school make fun of me and don't want me around. I worry about what's going to happen. I can't stay here too long, and I don't know if my dad will be able to take me

back. I go to see him once a month. He's got a drug problem and he's supposed to be getting help, but I don't think it's working. If he doesn't take me back, will I get moved to another foster home? Will I be adopted?

## The problems with foster care

Unfortunately the foster parent program has its problems. Even supporters of the system sometimes find it hard to be positive. Currently there are about 100,000 foster homes in the United States, and 350,000 foster children living in them. That means each house has three or four children. "It's painfully evident," says Gordon Evans, director of the National Foster Parent Association, "that many [homes] are overloaded." The program, he says, is "abundantly overwhelmed with removed children whose 'baggage' is heavy and challenging."

As dedicated to foster children as Evans is, he admits that "the program is in total chaos." There are simply too many children who need homes, and too few adults willing to offer them. Evans calls dedicated foster parents "earthbound angels," for they are put in charge of children with tremendous problems. Kids who have been taken from unsafe homes or moved from one foster family to another may have emotional problems that put severe stress on a foster family's resources and relationships. That is why many people decide not to provide foster care, and so the number of children waiting for good homes continues to grow.

The foster care program is overcrowded, understaffed, and underfunded. Although some claim that foster parents take in children merely as a way of earning money from the state, this is generally not true. In most cases the amount the state provides (an average of $350 per month) is not enough to support a child. And sad stories of abusive foster parents are again the exception. The majority of foster parents are kind, caring people. They have made many sacrifices in their own lives to help needy children, most of whom have so many problems they cannot appreciate what the foster parents are doing for them.

Another problem with the foster care system is bureaucracy: paperwork, legal forms and filings, government regulations. When foster parents and administrators are overburdened with these kinds of demands, their time and money cannot be put where it is most needed: on the kids. To ease the situation, shelters were set up where children could stay temporarily until long-term homes were found. The idea was good, but the result has been bad. Because there are not enough foster families, children often end up staying in the shelters for months rather than nights. Many shelters are now more like orphanages, with nearly one hundred beds, where children have become wards of the state. Without family ties and adequate personal care, their behavior and emotional problems grow worse, making them more difficult to place in foster homes or put up for adoption.

## The special problems of teenagers

Because foster care has a bad reputation, many children fear being placed in it and run away to avoid it. This happens more often with youths over age twelve. Many try to stay away from social workers, police, and others who might control their lives or put them into foster care. Counting these kids is impossible, but officials estimate that as many as two million teens are living alone on the streets without any adult caretaker.

How do teenagers end up in this situation? Some are runaways. They have run away from troubled homes where drugs, family violence, crime, or divorce created problems too big for them to bear. Others are throwaways, children who have been told to leave home by a parent or guardian. A national network that tracks homeless youths estimates that a third to a half of all homeless teens are throwaways who have been kicked out of their homes. Still others are those who started life as homeless children and have found no permanent place. When they get older they wander away from their families to live on their own. And some are kids who have run away from foster care or a group home, deciding they were better off by themselves.

*Officials estimate that nearly two million teenagers live alone on the streets. Many of these young people are runaways and throwaways who have left troubled homes or are avoiding foster care.*

Davonna was eleven when her parents divorced and she moved with her mother into a housing project. Her mother had a steady job, went to church, and tried to make a stable home. In junior high, however, Davonna started hanging out with a wild crowd, and by fourteen she was pregnant. Embarrassed and angry, her mother threw her out of the house and forbade relatives to take her in. Davonna became a throwaway. While she was pregnant she lived on her own, on the streets. Only days before her baby was born did she go to a women's shelter. There she got medical care and help, but she knows she can't live forever in the shelter. Davonna says she would give anything to go home to her mother, whom she still loves, but she doesn't know if that will ever be possible.

David was abandoned by his parents when he was three and sent to foster care. Over the next four years he lived in fourteen different foster homes. In the last home, he was sexually abused. By the time he was a teenager, David had decided to run away. Living on the streets, he fell into crime, drug dealing, prostitution, and poor health. Today David has leukemia and suffers from malnutrition. He sleeps in a city park when the weather is good; when it's bad, he goes underground to the train tunnels. "The doctors don't give me more than two or three years [to live]," he says, rather nonchalantly. "I really don't think about it. I'm busy looking for my next meal."

Because they are trying to avoid police, the courts, and social workers, homeless teens rarely go to shelters or food kitchens for help. They sleep on the street, in a park, or with other homeless people they meet. For food, they steal, beg, or rummage through dumpsters. Hunger is constant. In order to keep hidden they stay away from schools, and so they have little education. Health care is a problem, for it requires either money or registering with social services, which would lead to discovery.

Like Davonna, many homeless youths dream of returning to their parents or family. After months or even years on their own, some do try. But sadly, 80 percent end up back on the streets again in just a short time.

# 2

# Where Do Homeless Children Live?

After a while of living in a shelter you get on each other's nerves. You, like, go crazy, from being so close together all the time. We been here at this shelter almost two years now. There's four of us living in one hotel-size room. There used to be five, but my brother run away last month. We're lookin' for him, but I can tell you he'll never come back here to live. Why would you? I'll probably leave myself when I'm 15—if I'm not too scared.

TWELVE-YEAR-OLD Shaun is one of the 350,000 Americans who the government estimates sleeps in home-less shelters each night. More than half of these people are children and their families. The poorest are those who live in a single-parent family headed by the mother. Living in a shelter is better than sleeping on the street, say homeless kids—but not much. There are three kinds of shelters where children and their families can go. Some are not as bad as others, but none is a real home.

The first kind are welfare hotels, so-called because most of the families who live in them receive welfare payments from the government. These are private hotels, once com-fortable and attractive, perhaps, but over the years increas-ingly run-down and now often barely fit for living. The government pays the owners rent on the rooms where homeless families live.

The second kind are barracks-style shelters set up in large, unused buildings like schools or auditoriums. These

*Family-style shelters, usually run by private organizations, offer children and their families clean, private rooms. These shelters help families obtain food, health care, and education, and offer counseling services.*

shelters are usually run by the city. Cots are placed side by side in huge rooms, like an army barracks. Dozens of people sleep in the same room, and there is no privacy. Most barracks-style shelters allow single people to stay for only one night, but families with children may stay up to a week.

The third kind, family-style shelters run by private organizations like the Salvation Army, are among the best, but there are far too few of them. Not only do they have rooms with doors where families can have some privacy, but they are generally cleaner and not as run-down. Counselors and staff members help homeless children and their families obtain food, health care, education, and psychological counseling.

The average stay in a family-style shelter or welfare hotel is thirteen to sixteen months. In many shelters, fathers are not allowed to live with their children unless they are registered with the welfare office as being a member of the family. Often the mother and children receive more welfare money or benefits if the father is not an official family member. But if he is not registered, he cannot live with them in a welfare hotel or similar type of shelter. At

*A young girl huddles with her cat on the floor of a run-down hotel room. Welfare hotels provide homeless families with shelter, but the living conditions are often appalling.*

some places the father can go into the shelter to see his children only if he pays a fee each time he visits.

## Welfare hotels

The term "hotel" or the fact that the government pays tenants' rent at these shelters does not mean that they are nice places. Welfare hotels do not have fluffy white towels and clean sheets, or fresh paint and wallpaper on the walls. Welfare hotels are some of the most horrible "homes" on earth. They are too often run-down and overcrowded, riddled with mice, lice, cockroaches, and germs. Whole families often live in one room; two or three children may sleep in the same bed. Fortunate families have a hot plate on which they can fix simple meals, but since there is rarely a table, the family eats on the floor. Many hotels prohibit cooking in the rooms, so residents must depend on modest government meal vouchers to eat in restaurants. In some places broken plumbing or heating remains unrepaired. In others, residents have to ask for toilet paper and are lucky to get it. Drug dealers and prostitutes roam the halls, doing their illegal business in each other's rooms and fighting on the streets and sidewalks. Thirteen-year-old Missy didn't expect much when she heard she was moving to a welfare hotel, but what she found was even worse than she had expected:

When my mom told us we was going to live in a hotel, I thought it would at least be clean. But this place had holes in the walls and cockroaches was running everywhere. We had a bathroom but it didn't work, so we had to go up four flights, to the fifteenth floor, to use the bathroom. There was this big chunk of ceiling hanging down in our room and one night it fell on my baby sister who was sleeping in the bed with my mom. The next day my mom said, "That's it," and we moved out. We moved into a hotel on the other side of town where we live now. But this one ain't no better.

Despite the bad conditions, welfare hotels are not cheap. The government pays the landlords huge amounts of rent. The average cost per room per night is about seventy-five dollars, but some are much higher. At seventy-five dollars a night, monthly rent amounts to more than twenty-one hundred dollars. Many frustrated mothers have pointed out that if only the government would spend that money on renting a house or apartment for her family, the cost would be much less.

Often parents are afraid to speak out about the horrid conditions in welfare hotels. They know that if they argue with the hotel owner, their children may have no place to live the next night. Not surprisingly, most welfare hotels have a very bad reputation. Exposés in newspapers and on television have caused many of them to close. But until a better solution is found, closing the hotels only forces more homeless children and their families onto the streets.

## Barracks-style shelters

Barracks-style shelters are different from welfare hotels, but not much better. The inside of a barracks shelter is a sea of cots. Side by side, with only three feet between them, hundreds of people are crowded together each night. Family members push their cots close to make themselves a little island in this vast sea. Doing this adds a few more feet to the airspace that separates them from the next family. Babies, older children, parents, and single people all live together here.

Upon entering the shelter, each person is given toilet paper and toothpaste; mothers receive diapers for babies. The shelters have bathrooms, but to use them people must wind their way through the sea of cots. Finding their way back in the middle of the night can be hard for children. The shelter provides meals since there is no place for each family to cook. But often the meals are bad—sour milk, stale bread, and food that tastes like plastic.

Worst of all, there is no privacy. When babies cry or children play too loudly or adults argue, everyone is bothered. Not even the bathrooms have separate stalls in many shelters. "When you want to change clothes," says Fernando, "you have to get someone to hold a blanket for you." After nearly two years of homelessness, Fernando has gotten used to what he calls "living in a fishbowl. But for a long time," he says, "you have a creepy feeling."

## Family-style shelters

*Barracks-style shelters provide homeless people with meals and a place to sleep but offer no privacy. Inside, hundreds of cots are placed side by side so that the shelter can accommodate a large number of people.*

No shelter is a good solution to homelessness, but the nicest ones are the family-style shelters run by private organizations like churches or the Red Cross. These shelters offer more than just a place to stay. They provide services so children and their parents can help rebuild their lives. There are kitchens where older children or parents can cook meals. The rooms are clean and private, arranged like apartments, with doors that close for privacy.

Here, day care for younger children is provided and older kids are enrolled in school. Through the shelter, chil-

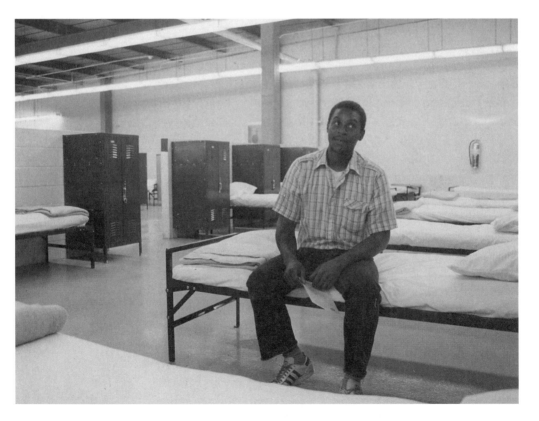

dren and parents can receive medical or mental health care. Older children can take part in classes where they learn how to manage a home or make out a budget. Shunda tells about a "rap group" for teens held once a week: "Kids get together and talk with a counselor about what's bothering us, what questions we have, you know. We talk about anything—birth control, drugs, gangs, school, whatever's on anybody's mind."

Most family-style shelters require residents to follow strict rules. Usually unmarried fathers cannot spend the night, but many shelters do allow a child's friend from outside the shelter to spend a night with him or her. There are curfews, or times when the people who live in the shelter must stay inside for the night and no more guests are allowed. Many shelter residents don't mind such rules; they say they feel safer because of them. "Only it's strange," says one girl who's lived in a family shelter six months. "Usually it's your parents who make the rules, who tell you what you can't do. Here, my mother gets told and has to obey, just like me."

*A youngster attends the day care program provided by a family-style shelter.*

A family-style shelter is the closest thing to "home" many children have ever known. For the first time, says Ali, it seems like he has a family—brothers, sisters, cousins, aunts:

> Everyone here tries to help. People are kind. They care about you. You can talk to them without being afraid. We play basketball or football together. When you need something, you borrow it from somebody else, but you always pay it back. At the hotel, you couldn't never do stuff like that. You were afraid you'd get knifed just going into your own room.

At family-style shelters, counselors help parents try to find jobs. If the adults need to learn new skills in order to get work, the shelter arranges for them to take classes and even provides child care while they are away. Older children are anxious for their parents to find work, for they realize getting out of the shelter depends on their parents' having a steady job.

When a family is ready for a home of its own, the shelter helps locate housing they can afford. Staff members work with parents and children while they are still at the shelter to help them get ready for the move. After they are on their own, a social worker visits to help with any problems.

## Homeless outside the shelter system

Very few of the homeless "street people" who spend their nights on park benches or sleeping on the sidewalks on pieces of cardboard are children. But this does not mean that all homeless children go to shelters. There are other options, but none of them are good.

Many children move in with an aunt, uncle, or grandparent. This arrangement may work for a while, but overcrowding may become a problem unless the house or apartment is quite large. The home gets dirty, people get on one another's nerves, and they begin to argue over every little thing. Most leases or rental agreements say that friends or family may visit for only a few nights. If they stay longer, the landlord has the right to evict everyone.

Another option is long-term camping. While this may sound like fun at first, camping out for a long time is not like being on vacation. It's very hard to cook every meal in a firepit. Some campgrounds have only cold showers, or no showers at all, and there is no place to do laundry. Bathrooms are usually outhouses that get dirty and smell when dozens of people a day are using them. And unless you live in the South, bad weather can make it uncomfortable or impossible to camp out in the winter.

Some homeless people resort to living in their cars. This is not a good solution, but for some families, it's the only choice. Naturally it's hard to find room for everyone to stretch out for the night, and there are no bathrooms. With no place to cook, children often go hungry or are forced to dig through dumpsters looking for food. Some states have laws that say people cannot live in their cars, and in many places overnight parking is not allowed.

When *Life* magazine discovered them, the Damm family of California was living in their car. After their story was published, sympathetic readers sent cash, toys, and

cars so they could move into an apartment of their own. But soon the money and gifts were gone and the family was back on the street. They then became "squatters"—homeless people who live in abandoned buildings without permission. Their "home" was a former pig ranch in the California desert. A sign over the door read "House of Pain," and a look around showed that the place was aptly named. It was filthy and had no electricity or running water. The parents were drug users and the children became victims of abuse and neglect. When the family was arrested for trespassing, the children were put into foster care. Their mother went to a shelter and their stepfather became a drifter.

Not all squatters are irresponsible. Some do try to fix up the building where they are squatting and make it into a home. In a city this might be an old government building, a toolshed, a garage, or a run-down tenement house. But

*A homeless child peers through the tattered blinds of an abandoned house. Many homeless families resort to squatting, or living in abandoned buildings without permission, although it is against the law in most areas.*

abandoned buildings can cost much more to repair than homeless people can afford, so it is a slow, frustrating process. Squatting is also against the law in most places. While some police officers will look the other way, many do decide to arrest the squatters.

It is sometimes easier for homeless families to become squatters in a rural area. Here they are not so visible and the police are not as likely to find or arrest them. Rural squatters usually move into barns, sheds, chicken coops, or abandoned houses.

## How long do children remain homeless?

Homelessness is not a short-term problem that can be corrected in a week or a month. Most children stay homeless for at least a year, some much longer. Finding permanent, affordable housing is very difficult. Some cities locate apartments for mothers and children who have been living in shelters for several months, but often the housing is in crime-ridden sections of cities or the buildings are badly in need of repair.

Because of the large number of homeless families, there are many fewer apartments than there are applicants. Mothers and children who are desperate to get out of the shelter system often settle for this bad housing. When their new "homes" prove intolerable, the families find themselves back in the shelter system again. Unfortunately, one of every three families who registers with a shelter has been in a shelter before. They are coming back into the system after having failed to make it on their own.

A child and his or her parents can try to break away from the shelter system by moving into subsidized housing. This is public or government housing—usually large apartment complexes—where the rent is paid in part or in full by the government. Many of these housing projects were built in the late 1950s and 1960s, but most are now quite run-down and many are being torn down. Unfortunately, few units are being built to replace them, and so the need for affordable housing increases. The waiting period for getting into subsidized housing can sometimes be years.

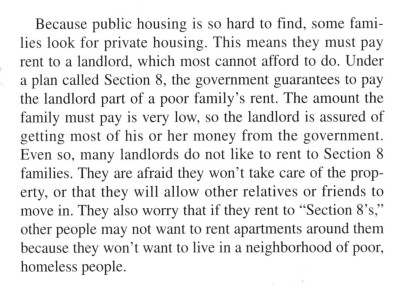

Because public housing is so hard to find, some families look for private housing. This means they must pay rent to a landlord, which most cannot afford to do. Under a plan called Section 8, the government guarantees to pay the landlord part of a poor family's rent. The amount the family must pay is very low, so the landlord is assured of getting most of his or her money from the government. Even so, many landlords do not like to rent to Section 8 families. They are afraid they won't take care of the property, or that they will allow other relatives or friends to move in. They also worry that if they rent to "Section 8's," other people may not want to rent apartments around them because they won't want to live in a neighborhood of poor, homeless people.

# 3

# Getting an Education

It messes you up to be changin' schools all the time. Teachers have different ways of teaching, and it takes a while to get used to each one. Then it's hard to make new friends every time you move, and to leave the old ones. This year I've been to three schools already. I started out at my home school. Then we moved in with my aunt and I went with her kids. When her landlord told us to leave, we moved into a shelter in the middle of the city, so now I go to Lincoln School. I don't like it, but what are you gonna do?

SIXTEEN-YEAR-OLD Anita likes school, and if she hadn't had to change schools three times in one year, she might have been a good student. But it's very hard to attend regularly and get good grades when you're homeless. Finding a quiet place to read or do homework at the shelter is almost impossible.

## Illiteracy and homeless kids

In the United States today, twenty-seven of every one hundred students drop out of high school. That figure is much higher than in many other countries. In Japan, for example, the dropout rate is only five students per hundred.

Many high school dropouts are homeless. Not having finished their education, they are often functionally illiterate, as well. This means they cannot read and write well enough to follow a recipe or fill out a job application. Without being able to read well, these young people will have few job choices. Those who do find work will not be well paid. On average, an illiterate adult's wage is only about half that of an educated person. More than sixty million Americans are now illiterate—and the number is increasing constantly.

Homeless children make up a large part of the dropout population because they have little encouragement from home, and are used to doing poorly in school. Half of them have repeated a grade and one-fourth are in special education classes. By their teenage years they are discouraged and ready to quit. Studies show that four of every ten homeless children are failing in school or working way below their grade level. Getting an education is not a top priority for many homeless kids. They are more concerned about where they will live, what they will eat, and if they will be attacked on the street.

## Starting out at a disadvantage

Children whose parents read to them when they were younger or help them now with homework, or insist that they turn off the TV when they're studying, are very fortunate. In homeless families, parents often have no time to read to children. They're too worried about finding food, money, and a place to live. Often they cannot read well themselves. Children who are living in shelters, cars, or campgrounds have no quiet places to study, no desk, and no reference books to help them with homework. Fourteen-year-old Doreen saw her marks go from A's in seventh grade to a C, D, and F when she moved to the shelter in eighth grade: "It was hard doing homework in the hotel because a lot of times there was too much noise and commotion. I'd tell Mom I did my homework, but I just wouldn't do it. . . . All I had was our one room, and people walking in and out at all times."

Statistics show that a child's home has much to do with how well he or she does in school. Children who have a quiet place to work, who do not have to worry about hunger or crime or poverty, children who go to school rested, well fed, and clean are much more likely to succeed than children who do not have these advantages.

Fewer than half of all homeless children are reading at or above their own grade level. Only a quarter are doing grade-level work in math. Among children with homes, the statistics are much better. Overall, 68 percent are reading at their grade level, and 57 percent are doing math at or above grade.

When a child has to repeat a grade, it means making a whole new set of friends, most of whom are younger and smaller. It can be very embarrassing to be called a "flunkie" or laughed at for being too big. Faced with such humiliation, many homeless kids decide just to drop out of school.

Low grades are only one of the education problems homeless children face. Many have trouble making friends at school. Without a home where they can invite children to play or eat or spend the night, they do not learn to get along with their peers. Younger children have problems sharing; older ones may pick fights. Many never form friendships and so school becomes a threatening place to which they don't want to go. In this environment, it doesn't take long for them to become loners and dropouts.

*Homeless kids often have difficulty concentrating on their homework when surrounded by the commotion of a shelter. These children usually receive little encouragement from their parents and have higher illiteracy and dropout rates than other kids.*

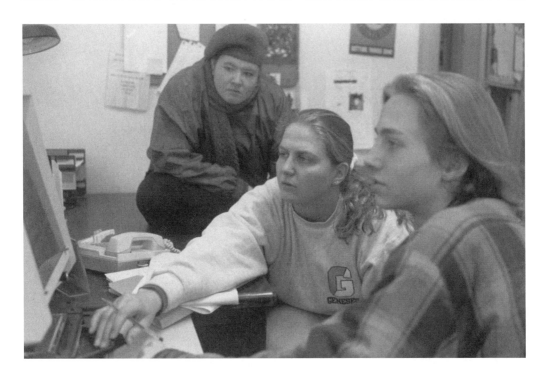

*A staff member of a homeless youth shelter helps a teen locate job listings on a computer. Finding work or shelter is often more important to homeless youths than attending school and receiving an education.*

Unfortunately, it's not just fellow students who can make life miserable at school. Some teachers simply do not have enough time in their school day to deal with kids who may not show up tomorrow. Nor do they have enough time to care for all the problems that homeless kids bring to school with them: acute and chronic illness, filth and hunger, exhaustion and stress. Says one New York teacher, "I've had three children and I've had forty-five. . . . I never know, from one morning to the next, who will be here or how many." Often, she says, her most important job is "calming the kids down." Because of their unstable lives, they are often angry at the world, and so may pose greater behavior problems than other children. They release their anger by "acting out," or misbehaving.

## Problems with attendance

Getting homeless children to attend school regularly is a big problem; there are too many reasons for not attending. One is that homeless mothers must take their children with them to the shelter when applying for a place to stay for the night. In order to be assigned a place, shelter officials must see every member of the family. Often the wait can take several hours. This may happen many times during the school year, sometimes more than once a week.

Parents who are moving from one shelter to another are not likely to enroll their children in school. Even if the child is enrolled, changing schools too often causes declining grades and poor performance. The new school may be slightly ahead of the old one, or teachers may use different methods, which can be confusing to students whose grades are already low.

In addition, more than half of all homeless kids suffer some type of mental or physical problem that keeps them from attending school regularly. Among children who are not homeless, that number is less than 20 percent.

Transportation is another roadblock to regular attendance. Often a child's shelter is a long way from the school. If busing is not available, most cities will pay for students to use public transportation. But the ride can be very long, and figuring out the transit system can be difficult for younger children. Not going to school at all is a much simpler option.

Teachers face a problem convincing homeless kids that an education will help them in life. Many homeless parents are dropouts themselves and don't see education as a priority. Older brothers or sisters may be involved in drug dealing or prostitution. This earns them big money but requires no education. Ignoring the huge risks, younger children may be drawn into this illegal, dangerous lifestyle.

## Shame

Most homeless children try hard not to let their classmates know they are homeless. They worry that other students will make fun of them or say mean things about their parents. But it's not a fact that's easy to hide. Some schools have special buses to transport shelter kids. These buses usually leave before the other students are dismissed, so it's obvious who is homeless. Raul, who is sixteen, tried walking instead of taking the bus, "but it was four miles, man, and after a few days I couldn't do it. My secret's out now. I'm one of the busers, but I live with it."

## Finding solutions for educating the homeless

At some schools homeless kids are put into separate classrooms. Though this may seem unfair, the students say they prefer it. Here they are no longer different from everyone else. They don't need to worry about being laughed at or ridiculed. The teacher understands their needs, and can help them with personal problems as well as schoolwork.

Salt Lake City, San Diego, and other U.S. cities have special schools for homeless children. They are located near welfare offices or homeless shelters, an easy walk for the children who will be using them. Salt Lake's is called the School with No Name and the teacher, Stacey Bess, says she is "in love with" the kids.

At the School with No Name, kids are made to feel welcome, no matter what their situation. In the corner of the classroom is a pillow bed for those who are too tired to stay awake. Children are encouraged to come to school every day, even if they are hungry or have no good clothes. "I have one boy in my class," says Bess, "who has only one set of clothes. Can you imagine him wearing them to a public school every day?" Bess uses "positive points" to inspire students to do well in her class. Children collect points for good work and exchange them for items like toys, music tapes, or curling irons.

A shelter schoolteacher in Tacoma, Washington, says she takes care of a child's "belly needs" before taking care of the "mind needs." A child cannot learn when he or she is hungry or tired, upset or afraid. Many times the teacher must act as a parent, friend, and counselor as well as an educator. At shelter schools, children are not punished for misbehaving in class or arguing with other students as they might be in public school. Teachers know that these kids have many social problems that cannot be handled in conventional ways. Part of their education is to learn appropriate behavior that will help them function well in society.

*At The Place, a shelter school for homeless teens in San Diego, young people are encouraged to continue their studies. Because The Place is smaller than a public high school, teachers are able to provide their students with individual attention and guidance.*

People who support separate shelter schools for homeless kids say their staffs understand their students' behavior and know how to handle it. Working with teachers who understand them and being surrounded by other students in the same situation makes it easier for kids to focus on learning. Shelter schools are generally small, so students get individual attention, something rare in public schools. Seventeen-year-old Deanna rides a city bus to a special shelter school in San Diego. She could attend a public high school closer to her shelter, but she prefers The Place, San Diego's school for homeless teens. "It's a lot better than regular school. I tried regular high school and I dropped out." The Place provides many services for homeless kids that are not available at a public high school, such as showers, a washer and dryer, a kitchen, donated clothing, even a doctor who checks new students for HIV and other infections.

## Shelter schools

Teachers like those at The Place, who work with the homeless, are usually very dedicated people. They care

*Homeless teens at The Place have access to facilities that are not available at public high schools, including a kitchen, showers, and a washer and dryer. Students can also receive donated clothing and can obtain medical examinations.*

about what happens to their kids, both in and out of school. "Being in school is the best thing in their lives," says one teacher. "If they were here more, we could help them more."

To bridge the gap between school and shelter, some communities have started afternoon programs for homeless kids. One of the most successful is Boys Harbor in New York City. After school a bus takes children to an old school building where they can play, do crafts or other activities, and have a snack. Teachers are available to help with homework, and the children can eat dinner before returning to their shelter. Most Boys Harbor participants like the program very much. "The kids at Boys Harbor are my only friends," says one. "The [shelter] is like living in the zoo."

Unfortunately there are too few places like Boys Harbor because there is not enough money. "In the long run," says one social worker, spending more money on such programs "will save dollars. These kids would get an education and not just drop out and become wards of the state later."

Sandy McBrayer, founder of The Place, believes in schools that stay open "seven to seven. . . . I want our schools to re-create the kitchen table," she says. "When I was a kid, you'd come home from school and do your work on the kitchen table and your parents would come and talk to you." Sandy knows this doesn't happen in a homeless child's family, so she tries to do it in her school. "I love all my kids and I think they're the coolest kids you'll ever meet," she says. The students feel the same way. "She's a really cool lady," comments Shawna. "There's no other school like this one. They feed you, they give you clothes, counseling. They help you get an education. You can't get no job without education, unless you sell dope, and I don't want that." In recognition of her success in educating homeless children, Sandy McBrayer was voted National Teacher of the Year for 1994.

*Teacher Sandy McBrayer helps a student with her schoolwork at The Place, the shelter school McBrayer founded for homeless teens.*

## A legal right to education

Since 1987, educating homeless children has become a state government responsibility, thanks to the efforts of the late Connecticut congressman Stewart B. McKinney. The so-called McKinney Act provides money and services not only for homeless education but for the welfare of homeless people in general. The purpose of the McKinney Act is "to provide urgently needed assistance to protect and improve the lives and safety of the homeless, with special emphasis on elderly persons, handicapped persons, and families with children." Under the act, "each child of a homeless individual and each homeless youth [will] have access to a free, appropriate public education." "Appropriate" means that a child will receive the same education offered to all public school students, including special help or classes for those with special needs. These needs might include facilities for handicapped kids, classes for students with limited English, programs for gifted and talented students, and more. The McKinney Act also requires school districts to change any rule that says a child must be a resident in order to attend school.

Thanks to Congressman McKinney, all fifty states are now required to protect homeless children's rights to equal and appropriate education. However, some people oppose this act. Because schools are funded largely by the tax dollars of those who live in the community, some neighborhoods say they cannot afford to educate children from outside their area. But people like Sandy McBrayer point out that a high percentage of criminals are school dropouts with little education. "It costs $30,000 a year to incarcerate [jail] someone and $4,500 to educate them," McBrayer says. She asks school administrators who want to turn away homeless children, Which is the better choice?

# 4

# Staying Healthy on the Streets

My mom and stepdad did crack and heroin all the time. They were always sharing needles around with their friends. When I was twelve, my stepdad learned he had AIDS. My mom was pregnant when he died, and she had it, too, but she didn't know it. When my little sister was born, she was an AIDS baby. For a while Mom was OK, but then the AIDS got to her. She spent a lot of time in the hospital, and was terrible sick. My little sister was put in foster care and I went to stay with my uncle who lives north of Houston. Every day I worried about my mother until finally we got the word that she died. It was terrible. I cry for her every night, but that don't do no good. I'm really worried about my sister; I don't ever see her.

LIKE ANYA'S LITTLE sister, homeless children's health problems often begin before they are born. Homeless women are less apt to seek or receive good prenatal care. In fact, 25 percent of all pregnant women in the United States receive very little or no prenatal care. This number is even higher among pregnant black women, four of ten of whom get no health care during the first three months of pregnancy. Not surprisingly, twice as many black babies die during their first year than do white babies.

An important part of prenatal care is eating right. A mother who does not eat well or take proper vitamins runs the risk of her baby's being anemic—having too few red blood cells. Anemic children are at a much higher risk for illness and health problems than are normal children. A mother's poor eating habits can cause low birth weight in the child. Babies who are born with a lower than average birth weight—under five pounds—run a much greater risk of physical and mental health problems as they age.

A greater number of homeless children are born with addictions to drugs or alcohol, or diseases like AIDS, syphilis, or gonorrhea, than are children from stable families. Even if they receive medical help after birth, there is a strong chance these children will suffer mental and emotional troubles or permanent damage to their nervous systems.

When children are born sick or addicted they may be kept in the hospital a long time. They become part of the group known as boarder babies because they "board" or stay at the hospital for months or even years. After birth, the mother leaves the hospital, but the baby remains. Most hospitals will not release a sick, addicted, or infected child to a mother who has no home and no way to care for the baby. Once the child begins to recover or loses its addiction, it becomes a ward of the state. The state is then re-

*Like many boarder babies, this newborn suffers from an addiction to crack cocaine. For the first months or even years of her life she will be homeless, living in the hospital and then in foster care or an institution.*

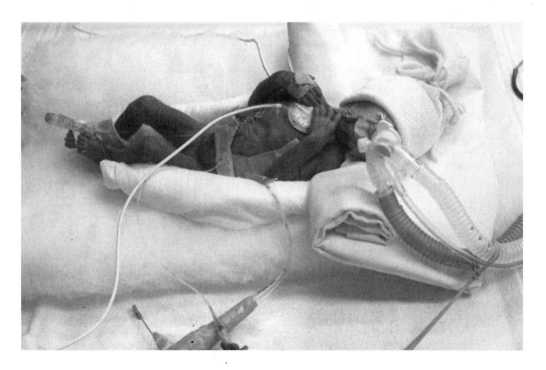

sponsible for finding a home for the child, either in foster care or in an institution.

Doctors say boarder babies suffer greatly from having had no home of their own and no parent to care for them during the first few months of life. The hospital has made them physically healthy, but they have suffered mentally and emotionally from having little affection or loving care. As they grow older, boarder babies are likely to be retarded or very slow to develop.

Another condition affecting homeless infants is known as failure to thrive. Affected children suffer from hunger, poor nutrition, and ill health, and do not gain weight as fast as they should. If left untreated, a child suffering from failure to thrive will die. Not surprisingly, the infant mortality rate (the number of babies who die compared to the number born) is high for homeless children. Among all Americans, 10.8 infants die for every 1,000 born. But among infants born to mothers living in welfare hotels in New York City, the infant mortality rate is 24.9 deaths per 1,000 births—more than twice as high.

## Hunger: A partner of homelessness

Hunger and poor nutrition are big contributors to the ill health of many homeless people. When a family is living in a welfare hotel, or in a car, or camping out for lengthy periods, it can be difficult or impossible to fix regular meals. The first problem is finding money to buy the food. But even when families receive food stamps or other food allowances from the government, they usually lack cooking facilities such as a stove or refrigerator. Sterilizing baby bottles or keeping formula refrigerated may be impossible, and so the risk of malnutrition or infection in homeless infants is very great.

Without cooking facilities, many homeless families buy ready-to-eat products. Foods like cookies, crackers, and pop, bologna and sugar cereals lack the nutrition of fresh meats, fruits, and vegetables. Ready-to-eat foods are often high in sodium, fat, sugar, and other ingredients that contribute to health problems.

*"SURE YOU'RE HUNGRY, BUT DON'T GO EATING ANYTHING HERE UNTIL MOMMA HAS CHECKED IT FIRST."*

Some families who cannot cook receive a meal allowance from the government in the form of coupons that allow them to buy food in restaurants, but often the amount is too small to buy a decent meal. So, too often the meal allowance is spent at a cheap fast-food restaurant where the food is low in nutritional value. Malnutrition is caused not only by a lack of food, but also by eating improper foods. A child who eats regularly but eats only chips, pop, or other junk food will suffer from malnutrition just as surely as will a child who has too little to eat.

Children who do not eat right face a lifetime of health problems. Malnutrition can be the cause of poor bone and muscle development, as well as of constant fatigue. These children are also more vulnerable to infection. Bone diseases like rickets or scurvy are caused by a lack of vitamins C or D in a child's diet. Too little riboflavin causes sores on the skin and in the corners of the mouth. Pellagra, a condition that brings on diarrhea, skin rashes, and mental problems, is caused by a lack of niacin. Low vitamin A can result in eye disease and poor vision.

Malnutrition is not the only health worry for homeless children. Living in dirty hotels and shelters, they are surrounded by health hazards. In recent years, lead poisoning caused by kids' eating peeling paint off the walls of welfare hotels has become a big health worry. Lead-based paint was banned many years ago, but it remains on the walls in many shelter rooms. Eating chips of this peeling paint can cause severe damage to a child's nervous system.

The government runs health care clinics where homeless children can be seen by a doctor free of charge. But in recent years lack of funds has closed many free clinics. Those that remain open may be several miles from the family's

*A homeless child waits to fill his bucket with water from a spouting fire hydrant. As a result of poor diets and unsanitary conditions, homeless children often become malnourished and suffer from health problems.*

shelter, making transportation a problem. The Salud Family Health Centers in Colorado serve many low-income families. Salud buses migrant and homeless children to central locations for dental, hearing, vision, and other health care needs. "We provide service to a tremendous number of patients," says one staff member, "but we all know our funds are in very short supply. We're losing many dedicated public health care providers because they just can't take the low pay any more. Those who are left are worried about losing their jobs. You can't blame them, but it's very sad." Underfunded and understaffed, government-subsidized health clinics cannot adequately meet the needs of thousands of poor and homeless people.

Without proper health care and medicine, and already in a weakened condition from hunger or malnutrition, homeless children may take a long time to recover from even simple illnesses. Because most of them do not get regular health care checkups, doctors may never detect conditions that could be corrected if treated early, such as poor eyesight or hearing loss.

## Illness stalks homeless young people

Another problem is neglect of immunizations. Most children receive regular shots in infancy to protect them from childhood diseases like measles, whooping cough, and mumps. But a homeless child who does not visit a doctor may never receive these immunizations, and so lives at higher risk for disease.

Homeless teenagers face an added health risk from involvement with drugs and alcohol. Addiction is only one of the dangers. Long-term use of drugs causes the body's immune system to function poorly. It is harder for a body already weakened by malnutrition, lack of immunizations, and wretched living conditions to fight off illness and infection. Kids who use needles to inject drugs into their bodies risk disease and even death from germs transmitted on the needles. Homeless teens also battle depression and suicide brought on by their seemingly hopeless living conditions and made worse by drug use.

Many homeless teenagers become prostitutes to earn money while living on the streets. This greatly increases their chances of contracting sexually transmitted diseases, particularly AIDS. It also creates another health problem: pregnancy. Any teenage girl runs health risks during pregnancy, but for a homeless teenager, those risks are greatly multiplied. The chances of problems in pregnancy are greater for girls under sixteen than for women in their twenties. Conditions like diabetes or anemia, which sometimes develop during pregnancy even in healthy women, can become major problems. If left untreated, as they often are in homeless women, they can cause low birth weight and stunted development in the newborn, leading to permanent mental or physical damage or even death.

## Mental health problems

Physical health is closely tied to mental health. When a child is having mental or emotional problems, he or she may also become physically sick. Most young children do not suffer from severe stress or depression, but homeless children are an exception. The psychological problems caused by not having a home, by seeing parents worried and depressed, being laughed at by classmates, or having too little to eat, can be overwhelming for a child, as it was for eleven-year-old Joey:

> My mom was always a nervous person. But after we moved into the shelter she got really bad. There was so much noise there—yelling and screaming, fights all the time. In the middle of the night you'd come flying awake with somebody yelling in the hallway outside your door. The stress really wears on your nerves. My mom, she started getting really bad headaches and pretty soon I was getting them, too.

Not knowing how to cope with the fears they are feeling, many homeless children take out their anxiety on themselves. One boy pulled out three of his permanent teeth. Another child ripped out big handfuls of her hair. Some kids stop eating, or throw up what they do eat. Other children take out their frustrations on society. They misbehave in school, act up in the shelter, get violent on

*Homelessness causes stress and suffering for the entire family, including the youngest members. Studies show that preschool children who live in shelters are often developmentally delayed and have trouble acquiring language skills and muscle coordination.*

the streets. Children who remain homeless for a long time may develop health problems like chronic upset stomachs, migraine headaches, or difficulty in breathing. Some may talk of suicide.

Most children do not blame their parents for their homeless situation. In fact, most are very defensive of their parents. They worry about their family's future and try to help, but there is little they can do. Too often their worry erupts into mental or physical illness.

Studies indicate that the stress and uncertainty of homelessness causes suffering even in young children. A recent study by Harvard University shows that more than half (54 percent) of preschool children who live in shelters suffer severe problems in development. The children in the study group were slower than children their age in acquiring language skills, muscle coordination, and personality and social development. Some would revert to crawling long after they had learned to walk. Such early problems set the stage for even bigger trouble when these children reached school age. Many suffered from depression and severe anxiety. Most admitted having had thoughts of suicide.

## What is being done to treat ill homeless children?

Government-funded health clinics treat the mental and physical problems of thousands of homeless children every day. But many more rarely or never get health care. Lack of transportation to a clinic, teenagers' fears of being discovered, parents' inability to fill out forms for their children—these and many other reasons keep homeless kids from getting the health care they need. Because homeless families move so often, keeping medical records up-to-date and getting regular health care checkups is almost impossible.

When a homeless child has a severe illness, it can be impossible to receive good long-term care. In a shelter it is very hard to get the rest so necessary for recovery. When it's time for medication, parents may not be available to help their children or may not understand how the drug is to be taken. There may be no clean place to change bandages or dressings or no refrigerator to store medicine.

Living with constant pain or illness is in itself discouraging and depressing. Homeless children may give up hope that their situation will ever get better. Homeless teenagers are among the first to give up hope. Most of them are very aware of the health risks posed by prostitution, drug use, AIDS, and alcoholism. But all too often they ignore the risks, not because they think problems like this will never happen to them, but because they don't care. Many have given up on life; it doesn't matter to them whether they live or die. Fifteen-year-old Alfredo is one of them:

> Some of my street friends were shootin' this heavy duty speed and they were pushin' me to try it. I knew all the bad buzz about AIDS and that, but I didn't care. You get that way on the street; you don't care. Speed's fun, it makes you feel good, so what the hell. You can just as easy die tomorrow from somethin' else. Around here anybody can get blown away any time, you never know. So, hey, go for it!

# 5

# Daily Life for a Homeless Child

JULIENNE, THE ELDEST of three children, was fourteen years old when her family became homeless. With her brother Leon, age nine, Julienne shared the care of their three-year-old brother, Bo. The family's problems began after Bo was born and their father, Donovan, got abusive. Rosy, the children's mother, put up with Donovan's beatings because she knew she couldn't support her family alone. But the night he smashed Julienne in the face and broke her nose, Rosy left with the kids.

For several weeks the family stayed in an emergency shelter run by the city. Every night Rosy gathered the children around on her cot in the big hall where they slept with a hundred other people and read to them from the Bible. Julienne wasn't sure if her mother could really read or if she just knew the stories by heart, but the words were soothing at a time when the girl was more scared than ever before in her life.

After several weeks a social worker at last brought good news. There was a motel room available for fifteen dollars a night, which would be subsidized by the government. Rosy was delighted to leave the shelter, but the kids hated their new "home." It was very small—a single room with two double beds, one for the boys and one for Julienne and her mother to share. Social workers who spoke with or assisted the family pick up their story.

After about four months in the motel, Julienne became extremely lonely and depressed. The longer the family

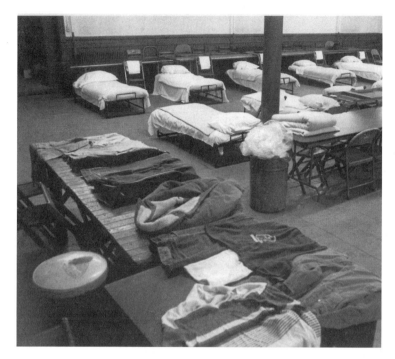

*Even though an emergency shelter provides refuge from the streets, it is not a permanent solution to homelessness. Most homeless children and their families travel from shelter to shelter until they find a welfare hotel or permanent housing.*

lived there, the smaller the room seemed to get. When they had lived in the apartment with their father, the boys had their own room with a door they could close. But in the motel, everyone lived on top of one another.

Every morning at 5:30, Rosy walked a mile and a half to her job as an aide at a nursing home. For a while Julienne and Leon took turns going to school so that one of them could stay at the motel with Bo. But when the social worker learned what they were doing, she arranged for Bo to go to day care. The day care was so far away that the little boy had to take a bus, and he was very scared. Next year, the social worker promised him, a new school for homeless kids would be opening closer to the motel. Leon and Julienne could go there, and it would have a preschool and day care center that Bo could attend.

When Julienne first heard about the new school she was upset. She didn't like the idea of leaving her friends. But as time passed she realized she had drifted further and further away from them since she moved to the motel. Her life was no longer like theirs. At first she had tried to hide from her friends the fact that she was homeless, but now she no longer cared. She had more practical problems on her mind.

One of those problems was clothing. Julienne had only two outfits for school. One was a very worn denim jumper; the other was a sweatshirt and a pair of jeans with big holes in the knees. When Rosy made extra money working overtime, she took the children to Goodwill and bought them each a new piece of clothing. But since those clothes were already used, they wore out faster than new ones. Each child had one pair of shoes provided by the social worker. Julienne didn't like hers much; they were white and looked like nursing shoes, but she didn't complain. Leon had a pair of boots that were too hot in the summer but would keep his feet warm and dry in winter and spring.

Because she earned so little at the nursing home, Rosy qualified for food stamps. Without a refrigerator, however, the family had no way to keep things cold except to put them on the window ledge in winter. Nor could they cook; the motel didn't allow hot plates in the room because of fire danger. In fact, all food was banned for fear it would attract rats and mice, but Rosy cheated a little on that rule. She used her food stamps to buy things like bread, cheese, peanut butter, fruit, and vegetables that didn't need to be cooked. Once a week she would bring home leftover rolls, half eaten boxes of cereal, and other foods that the nursing home was throwing away.

On days when there was nothing in the room to eat, Leon and Julienne had breakfast at school and took the extras home to Bo. The cafeteria served free meals to children whose parents were too poor to pay. It was embarrassing to hear your name called by the cafeteria worker and the "no charge" that followed. But it was worse to feel that constant, gnawing hunger in your stomach.

## Worry and anxiety

At first when they moved to the motel, Julienne was afraid. Central Avenue was a rough part of town. She worried about what she would do if a stranger came to the room while her mother was gone. But after a couple of months, life got so boring that Julienne actually hoped someone *would* stop by. Day after day the routine was the same. Rosy left before daylight; the kids got up a little later. On weekends Julienne and Leon took Bo to the park or to a mall about ten blocks away to window-shop. Sometimes they played baseball with a two-by-four they found on the street, using pine cones from the park as balls. On cold or wet days they watched TV on the old three-channel black-and-white set in the motel room.

Boredom wore on Julienne's nerves. With so much time to think, she began to brood about the future. She knew

*Children play amidst piles of garbage at a deserted apartment building. Homeless children sometimes become depressed and withdrawn out of frustration and boredom.*

she was lucky not to be sleeping on the street, but she wanted more from life than a dumpy motel room. She knew it was crazy to worry about things that might never happen, but she did it anyway. She asked the social worker questions: What if her father found them? What if her mother lost her job? What if they got evicted from the motel? What if her mother got really sick? But the social worker told her not to "borrow trouble."

Julienne worried about Leon, too. He had become disruptive in school and often picked fights with his classmates. The social worker promised to talk with Leon. At first the boy would say nothing to her, but finally he admitted that he was sick of the other kids' making fun of him. He was tired of them saying he had "dwebe" shoes and that he smelled like a garbage truck. Screaming and crying, he told the social worker he hated his life.

On Sundays, Rosy and her family went to church not far from the motel. Julienne liked the minister's strong, firm voice. She wanted to believe in God as much as her mother did. She could see what great comfort Rosy's faith gave her. But faith didn't work for Julienne. She kept telling herself that if it did any good to pray, her mother's life would be better by now. If God really cared, he would do something about their situation. But for her mother's sake, Julienne kept going to church, and kept begging God to listen.

## Living in a violent neighborhood

In time, though Julienne never cried or complained, the social worker noticed that she was becoming more and more withdrawn. Rosy told her the girl was depressed. One of the things she missed was going out with friends on Friday nights, even though she didn't have any money to spend. Since they moved to the motel, going out at night was simply too dangerous. Drug dealers lived all around. Julienne had heard drunks fighting in the alley and the sounds of gunfire just a block from the motel.

One time the motel security guard gave Leon five dollars to deliver a small package to a room on the back side of the motel. Julienne remembered how proud he was when he showed their mother the money. But Rosy was not at all proud. That night after Bo was asleep, Rosy made Leon and Julienne sit on the edge of the bed while she talked about drugs and dealers. First she scolded Leon; then she reminded him that he must never take money or favors from a stranger, no matter what the reason.

Leon suggested that if his mother knew people were dealing drugs right at the motel, perhaps they should tell the police. But Rosy said absolutely not. They might lose the only home they had. Chances were, the motel owner was part of the drug ring, and if he knew Leon was a "talker" the boy might be hurt—or even killed.

## On the streets as a homeless teen

From then on, Leon grew more and more depressed. Day after never-ending day of hunger and mess, sickness and crime, boredom and gloom had left both older children quiet and somber. Bo was sick much of the time; he never seemed to get over one illness before he caught another. His behavior was getting bad, too. Many days he just sat and banged his head on the wall of the motel room. It made Julienne depressed to watch him.

Then one day she had a terrible idea. Even though she told no one about it at the time, her social worker later pieced together Julienne's plan to run away. "No doubt she figured it would be one less mouth for her mother to feed," the social worker later said sadly, "one less problem for her to deal with."

Throughout the spring and summer Julienne collected cans to recycle, walking the streets with Bo to find them. By September she had saved fifty-seven dollars, and she was ready. With Leon and Bo safely registered in the new school, fifteen-year-old Julienne walked to the Greyhound station without saying good-bye to her mother. With some of her money she bought a bus ticket to a nearby town.

Her first night there was terrifying. "Bed" was a chair at the Greyhound bus station where she slept in fifteen-minute catnaps. The next day she planned to apply for a

*Many homeless teens run away because they think their absence will make life easier for their families. Sadly, these runaways find that they cannot provide for themselves and many resort to prostitution and crime.*

job at a fast-food restaurant. But the application asked for address and phone number, and Julienne had neither. Everywhere she went, the questions were the same.

The next two weeks were one continuous, exhausting blur. Julienne walked the streets, but without her earlier enthusiasm or confidence. Her dreams were dying fast and her new goal was merely to stay alive. She knew she had to do something quickly. Her money was running out, even though she had limited her expenses to three dollars a day.

Wandering the streets, Julienne met other kids like herself. Some invited her to stay with them in an abandoned building they had outfitted with old sleeping bags and couch pillows. Julienne accepted, glad for the chance to stretch out and sleep. But when she got to "base," as the kids called it, she found drug paraphernalia everywhere. In a growing panic Julienne watched her new friends get high—dusted, they called it. They asked her to join them, but she said no thanks, trying hard to be casual and offering the excuse that she needed to get some sleep.

As she lay in the sleeping bag, Julienne realized that she had a weapon the rest of these kids didn't have: her strong sense of self-worth. She, Julienne, didn't do drugs. She never had and she never would. She refused to try anything that would ruin her mind or body. On that, she was firm.

## Earning a living when you can't get a job

When Julienne awoke a few hours later, someone was in the sleeping bag beside her. Terrified, she crawled out and edged toward the door. Sensing her fear, an older woman sidled over and motioned for her to sit down. The woman talked in a tone that Julienne found confident and reassuring, telling her not to worry about money or a place to stay. As long as she stayed with them, the woman said, everything would be all right.

She then motioned to an older man she called John Boy, explaining to him that Julie needed to make some money and telling him to "set her up." John Boy smiled and began stroking Julienne's back, talking in the same reassuring tones. Julienne listened, stunned, as the reality of her situation hit her full in the face. Of course, John was a pimp and she was about to become a prostitute. She couldn't! She wouldn't! And then Julienne asked herself how she expected to make money any other way.

Over the next few months, Julienne provided "company" for countless men on countless evenings. It was a bad life—a horrid life—but at least she was making some much-needed money. Then, halfway through her fifteenth year, she started getting sick every morning. Sometimes the vomiting was violent; sometimes she could barely stand on her feet. Tracy, a girl she had met through John, told her she was probably pregnant, and that she should get a test at the clinic. But she must be careful, Tracy reminded her, to tell the clinic staff she was eighteen so that no one asked questions about her parents or family.

A few days later a doctor at the clinic confirmed Julienne's worst fear: her baby would be born in six months. John Boy was furious and screamed at her to get out of his sight. Terrified, Julienne ran until she came to a park. Here, under cover of the thick branches of a huge spruce tree, she cried until darkness overcame her. At that moment, all she wanted was to be back with her mother, Bo, and Leon in the boring old motel room, even for just one night. But that was impossible. What would Rosy do with her now?

For the next five months, Julienne wandered the streets, spending occasional nights in shelters for homeless women. No one questioned how old she was; she had aged to the point where her face looked older than eighteen. Thoughts of suicide crossed her mind as she wondered how she was going to support a baby when she couldn't even support herself. Death now seemed like a wonderfully simple solution.

It was in this mood that Julienne decided to go back to her family. She wouldn't ask Rosy to take care of her; she

only wanted to see her mother again and talk to her. But the motel was thirty-two miles away and she was nearly eight months pregnant, her belly swollen uncomfortably. She had no money left for a bus ticket, so she decided to hitchhike.

## Dead at sixteen

The next evening Julienne stood before her brothers' school, which was dark for the night. The motel was only two blocks away. Part of her was tremendously excited, but part of her was very scared. She could feel her heart pounding loudly in her chest as she walked up to the door of motel room number 21.

The window was dark and the curtains were drawn; probably the kids were watching TV. Julienne knocked and waited for the door to open—but it didn't. She knocked again; no one answered. Her fear mounting, she walked to the manager's office to ask about her family. A gruff, dirty man sat in front of a portable black-and-white TV. He growled when Julienne walked in, and asked what she wanted. When she explained that she was looking for her family in room 21, the man waved her off. He told Julienne that her family had left at least three months ago when they couldn't pay the rent and he had no idea where they had gone.

Julienne slept that night on a bench in the park where she and Leon used to take Bo to play. The next morning she got to Bo and Leon's school early, before any kids arrived, hoping the teacher had news of her family. But here the answer was the same. No one seemed to know what had happened to them. Trying to be helpful, the teacher wrote down the address of the agency where Julienne could find their social worker.

Though she was very tired and discouraged, she decided to walk there. But when at last she reached the office, she was told the social worker wouldn't be in that day. The office staff asked if Julienne could come back the next day. When she shook her head no, another social worker offered to see her. This woman knew little about the family's case, but she was willing to listen, and Julienne poured out her entire story.

When Julienne was through, the social worker told her that the agency had no address for her mother. They had lost contact about two months earlier. But she knew their case worker would want to talk with her. She urged Julienne to come back the next day. The woman offered to find her a bed in a shelter for the night, but politely Julienne lied, saying she'd stay with some friends.

Julienne never went back to the agency. One week later, police found her body on a bench in the park. She was unconscious but alive, apparently the victim of a drug overdose. The officer called for an ambulance to rush her to the hospital, where an emergency team delivered her baby and saved his life, but it was too late for Julienne. She was dead at sixteen, perhaps by suicide, perhaps by unintentional overdose of the drugs she had vowed never to take. After several months in the hospital, Julienne's son was at last turned over to social services. If he's lucky, he will be adopted; but many boarder babies are not. Their problems are simply too daunting.

# 6

# What Is Being Done for Homeless Children?

She would be like every other 12-year-old, going to school and everything, but at night . . . she slept on the floor instead of in her bed. She said, "When the lights go off, all of these thoughts keep coming into my head and I can't go to sleep."

"THESE THOUGHTS," EXPLAINS Jo Blum, director of Denver's Families First crisis center, were of sexual abuse by the boyfriend of the girl's mother. The child had no safe home when Families First intervened and gave her a place to stay while they helped find her a permanent, stable home. Thanks to Families First, the twelve-year-old is now in the custody of her grandmother in Kansas. When she left the agency she wrote a thank-you note, Blum recalls. "It said, 'We are all family in some way.'"

Notes like these are powerful, and oftentimes the *only*, thank-yous received by Jo Blum and the staffs of hundreds of other agencies across the United States that help homeless kids. Some agencies are run by the state or federal government. Many others, like Families First, are private. Some are independent agencies located in a single city; others have several offices throughout a region or across the country.

Government programs often focus their efforts on families, rather than children, and toward people living at or be-

66

© Boileau/Rothco. Reprinted by permission.

low the poverty line, rather than just the homeless. Staff
members say their programs are not as effective when they
serve only children. "We have found that if we help only
the child, we just put a temporary fix on the problem," says
one Colorado social worker. "Unless we work with the entire family, a homeless child's problems will not be solved
long-term." This is particularly true of housing. The government offers many types of housing assistance plans to
aid low-income and homeless families, but few of these
plans are directed just at children. The biggest exception is
government-run foster care, which provides homes or shelters for homeless and runaway or throwaway kids.

## How government agencies help

Agencies that provide welfare and food assistance often
make no distinction between homeless kids and children
from low-income families. The Department of Agriculture
program WIC (Women, Infants, and Children), for example, offers homeless and needy children up to age five nu-

tritional food supplements. The Commodity Supplemental Food Program (CSFP) serves children up to age six—not just homeless but all low-income kids. Aid to Families with Dependent Children (AFDC) is a federal and state program that offers food assistance to single-parent families "in which a needy child has been deprived of parental support." Certain states have "special need allowances to shelter families who are homeless or to prevent homelessness."

In the area of education, homeless children benefit more directly from government programs. The Department of Education sponsors Education for Homeless Children and Youth. Under this plan, federal money is given to the states "to ensure a free and appropriate education for homeless children" of all ages. The Department of Health and Human Services (HHS) serves homeless preschoolers through its Head Start program, along with children from low-income homes.

The Child Support Enforcement Program is a joint effort among federal, state, and local governments to enforce the collection of child support money from an absentee parent.

*Preschoolers from low-income or homeless families can participate in Head Start, a government program that helps prepare youngsters for school.*

Broadly designed to help any child with a "deadbeat" parent, the program very often ends up helping homeless kids. "Receiving child support payments," says the Interagency Council on the Homeless, "may enable some families to avoid homelessness or welfare dependency."

HHS also runs three programs specifically for homeless children. The Homeless and Runaway Youth Program provides federal funds to crisis centers that offer assistance to homeless kids. The money is used to help children solve the problems that have led them into homelessness and to reunite runaways with their families. The Transitional Living Program for Homeless Youth provides services to homeless kids "who cannot return to their homes and who have no safe alternative living arrangements." Youths in this program receive health care as well as training and experience in basic life skills, education, job skills, and other areas that will help them be self-sufficient and prevent dependence on welfare. And the Drug Abuse Prevention Program for Runaway and Homeless Youth deals with both alcohol and drug abuse among homeless kids, and offers counseling to them as well as to their families.

## Help from private organizations

Homeless children whose families need a clean, safe shelter often find better accommodations through private organizations than they do in government-supported shelters or public housing. The Red Cross, the Salvation Army, and local churches and rescue missions are some of the leading private organizations helping homeless children and their families. "It wasn't many years ago that children were a rarity at rescue missions," says Stephen Burger, executive director of the international Union of Gospel Missions. "Today they're the norm. . . . The idea of [the homeless being] old, alcoholic male drifters passing through a community is now a proven myth." Lorraine Minor of the City Union Missions in Kansas City, Missouri, blames the breakdown of the family on the increased numbers of homeless kids. Today, she says, "Children are being born into homelessness."

To accommodate the growing numbers of children and families, many private shelters are being designed like communities, utilizing residents' skills to maintain or improve the building and grounds and daily routines. Teenagers are trained to do repair and maintenance work or run errands. Preteens baby-sit younger shelter children while their parents help in other ways. By working together and drawing on one another's skills, shelter people build a sense of pride in themselves and their community. Without the burden of government paperwork, private shelters have more flexibility to try novel approaches.

A new type of shelter that has attracted both praise and criticism is one that limits certain kinds of aid to particular residents. At such shelters, people who show a desire to raise themselves out of their situation receive better food and more plush accommodations than the chronic homeless. One such shelter is St. Vincent de Paul Village in San Diego. "I just can't help all [homeless people] the same

*Homeless people enjoy a Christmas Eve dinner at the Salvation Army in Seattle, Washington. Private organizations like the Salvation Army provide homeless children and their families with clean, safe shelters and hearty meals.*

way," says Joe Carroll, the Catholic priest who founded St. Vincent's. So the newly homeless and those who are willing to work hard to better themselves eat swordfish and Haagen-Dazs ice cream while their children build sand castles in a colorfully painted playground. The chronic homeless sleep in a barracks-style dormitory with bunk beds and fewer services. Each day, St. Vincent de Paul's is home to 120 children: Father Carroll prefers to separate the long-term homeless from the young people at the shelter. Across the street from the shelter, children of all ages attend school with teachers who care deeply about them. Father Carroll has been criticized by some for not treating all homeless people the same way. But even his harshest critics say, "With children, he performs miracles."

In New York City, the largest provider of transitional housing and services for homeless children and their families is an organization called Homes for the Homeless. Since it was started in 1986, the group has served nearly twenty thousand children in need, from infants to teenagers. At any one time, approximately five hundred children under the age six live in housing provided by Homes for the Homeless. In addition to providing housing, HFH sponsors an educational program, called Jump-start, that has been much more effective in preparing children for school than traditional preschool and child care facilities. Parents are encouraged to participate in Jump-start with their children, so they develop a feeling for the importance of education. When parents are involved, they are more likely to encourage and support their child's education.

## Homeless teenagers find help at Covenant House

One of the largest and most successful private shelters for runaway kids is Covenant House. Begun in 1969 in New York City, it now has several branches in the United States, Canada, and Central America. Covenant House attracts teenage runaways and throwaways who are living on the streets. At night, volunteers drive around in vans, offering food and shelter to homeless kids. Some kids return with the workers to Covenant House, where staff members help them reunite with their families, register for foster care, or get into school or a job training program.

No one under twenty-one who asks to be admitted to Covenant House is ever turned away. "I know many youth desperately search for hope and the chance to have a trouble-free life," says Vincent Gray, executive director of Covenant House. "Given a warm structured setting, an accepting attitude and discipline, our young people can arrive at adulthood successfully."

One of many programs at Covenant House is "Rights of Passage," for young people ages eighteen to twenty-one. These youths serve as apprentices to major construction, building mainte-

nance, and real estate businesses. The companies run training courses and make a commitment to hire graduates after they finish training. In 1994, when he arrived at Covenant House, Mark had only the clothes on his back. Thanks to the ROP program he now has a good job, an apartment, and is taking night classes at a college.

Each year, more than a million homeless kids call Covenant House looking for help, a place to stay, a warm meal, or just a word of encouragement. Fifteen-year-old Rick is one of them. Rick ran away from home after one of many fights with his parents, determined never to go back. Hitching a ride on an eighteen-wheeler, he found himself several hours later at a truck stop with only a few dollars in his pocket. When he called Covenant House, volunteers came to his rescue.

Sixteen-year-old Monica is also one of the "saved." In a single year, she lost both her parents and was sent to a foster home. After being bounced from home to home for

*Teenage runaways and throwaways living on the streets can find solace at Covenant House, a private shelter that helps teens reunite with their families, register for foster care, or enroll in school or job training programs.*

more than a year, she decided to run away to the big city, but soon found herself lost and alone. Another runaway she met on the streets told her about Covenant House and she decided to call.

A sixteen-year-old Staten Island boy is another who owes his life to Covenant House. Although he was employed by Dunkin' Donuts, he had no home. He had not seen or talked to his mother in more than a year, and his father had died of AIDS four years earlier. When Covenant House picked him up, he was living on the street and contemplating suicide.

Some twelve hundred kids a night seek shelter in the New York center alone. One of the strongest forces at the center, Covenant House kids agree, is director Sister Mary Rose McGeady. "She'll only have met you once," says eighteen-year-old Christine Stewart, "and will always remember your name. She'll ask you how your day was and really want to know."

"I believe very deeply in what I do," says Sister McGeady. "If you treat kids right, respect them, it's a rare kid you can't help. They need someone to listen to them and give them positive reinforcement."

*Sister Mary Rose McGeady, the director of Covenant House, is the driving force behind the shelter's success.*

## Los Angeles Youth Network

Not as large as Covenant House, but very successful on the West Coast, is the Los Angeles Youth Network. LAYN operates a twenty-bed, sixty-day long-term shelter for homeless youths between ages twelve and seventeen. At LAYN's Drop-In Program, kids can get help during the day, even if they do not choose to spend the night. Because of its seventeen-year-old age limit, the program is the only one of its kind in Los Angeles specifically for minors. Seventeen-year-old Garrett is one of those helped by LAYN:

> When I was six years old . . . my parents got a divorce, and that's what screwed me and my brother up. . . . For years [my mother] did cocaine like two or three times a month. . . . Then all of a sudden when I was thirteen— wham. . . . She was wasted all the time. . . . [My mom and stepdad] spent all our money on [drugs]. When I was fourteen we got evicted 'cause they couldn't come up with the rent. So we moved into a friend's house. . . .

> Me and my brother didn't have no home, you know, so hookin' up with the gang gave us something to belong to. I'll tell you this, what makes kids get into gangs is parent neglect. The parents are never around; they're not helping you with your homework, or making sure you do it, or taking you to do things—that's why kids join gangs; so they can belong to something. And we're talkin' 'bout a lotta kids.

Each year LAYN serves ten thousand meals. It also provides counseling, tutoring, medical care, clothing, and transportation. Opened in 1986, the shelter regularly has to turn away kids for lack of room. At present, more than 40 percent are under fifteen. More than half suffered physical or sexual abuse at home. LAYN has a good track record. Nearly 80 percent of the kids who go there eventually return to live with their own families, go to foster or group homes, or live independently after age eighteen. Its mission, say LAYN directors, is "to end homelessness one kid at a time."

## Boys Town

One of the most famous organizations helping homeless children is Father Flanagan's Boys Town, founded just

*When Boys Town was founded in 1917, its first residents were destitute, homeless orphans.*

west of Omaha, Nebraska, in 1917 by Father Edward J. Flanagan. At Boys Town—an actual town with its own zip code—there are seventy-six long-term residential homes for both boys and girls. Today there are also Boys Town facilities in fifteen other locations around the country.

Boys Town offers many, many services for homeless and troubled kids, including short-term shelters, family counseling, a resource and training center, a hospital, and a high school. Its purpose is to provide food, clothing, shelter, education, spiritual guidance, and medical care to homeless, neglected, and abused children.

In one recent year, Boys Town provided direct care and treatment to 24,000 children and helped 575,000 more through its toll-free Boys Town National Hotline. Brandon, a fourteen-year-old boy from Maryland, is one of those who called the hotline. Brandon had run away from home to visit the grave of a high school friend who had died in a car accident. He told the hotline counselor he kept a knife under his pillow and had recently been in the hospital for treatment of depression. Now he was desperate again. Thanks to the hotline, Boys Town counselors came to Brandon's rescue with care and treatment.

Most of the children helped by Boys Town are between the ages of nine and nineteen. About 60 percent are boys. Its director, Father Val J. Peter, says Boys Town is "the only official village in the nation created exclusively for children in need of a fresh start in life."

## Hotline help

Another organization that provides advice and counseling to hundreds of thousands of teenagers every year is Youth Development International. Started in 1959 in New York, YDI now reaches across the country through its youth crisis hotline. Hotline volunteers can give young callers immediate help in the areas of protection, shelter, food, or counseling. The hotline serves as a national clearinghouse for more than seventeen thousand youth and social services. After so many years of assistance to kids in need, YDI has compiled an interesting profile of young people in crisis. Sixty percent are female, eighteen-year-olds being at greatest risk. For boys, seventeen is the highest risk age. Eighty percent of the kids who call for help are runaways who have been gone from home fewer than

*Today, the Boys Town compound in Omaha, Nebraska, provides homes for both boys and girls. Here, homeless and troubled youths can try to rebuild their lives.*

ten days. Nearly half have traveled fewer than ten miles. One quarter have fathered children or are pregnant. Three quarters of teens say they have a poor or nonexistent relationship with their parents. And saddest of all, 90 percent of the kids feel that life is hopeless.

## Kids helping kids

People who work with homeless children every day say the most important requirement is caring. Too often, people distance themselves from the homeless. They think of them as statistics and give them labels instead of names. It's easy to overlook the problems of a number or a statistic. But when a name and face—a real person—is suffering, it is much harder to ignore the problem.

Adults and large organizations aren't the only ones who can care. There are many ways that teenagers or younger children can help homeless kids. As part of a group, young people can help raise money to benefit homeless children. In Massachusetts, a group called Kids Helping Kids made patchwork pillows with the signatures of such national celebrities as Bill Cosby, Bill and Hillary Clinton, and David Letterman. They chose pillows to show that thousands of American children have "no place to rest their heads." When the pillows were finished, Kids Helping Kids held a pillow auction at a fancy hotel in Boston. The group raised several thousand dollars from bidders, which it donated to a nearby family homeless shelter.

But a person doesn't need to belong to a group in order to help homeless kids. People can show they care simply by being friendly to homeless young people. They can make a commitment not to ignore or make fun of homeless kids in school. And they can follow through by talking to them, eating

*When people take the time to get to know a homeless child or family, they can help ease the suffering of the homeless while making new friends.*

lunch with them, getting to know them, or inviting them to join an activity after school. For many homeless children, knowing that they have a friend or fit into a group is enough to encourage them to continue going to school.

For a child who has no permanent home, going home with a friend after school to play or have dinner can make him or her feel wanted, something very lacking in the lives of many homeless kids. Simple things like watching TV together, playing a game, or just sitting around talking can give a homeless child hope for a better life and a more positive outlook for the future. The barrier of isolation can be broken by smiles and friendly words.

People who care do not ignore or mock a homeless child's situation. Instead, they listen when the children talk, help out when asked, and generally try to be a friend. Sadly, too many children in this country spend each night hungry, cold, and lonely because too many people figure homelessness is somebody else's problem.

# Appendix

## What you can do to help homeless children

Young people who care about homelessness can help by getting to know a homeless child or family. Volunteer at an agency or shelter, or simply be a friend to a homeless child at school. Sparing a couple of minutes to talk to a family or child can do much to brighten their day.

The book *What You Can Do to Help the Homeless* has dozens of excellent ideas for young people. Some volunteer individually; others help as part of a school, religious, athletic, or scouting group. Here are some ways young people can help:

• Tutor homeless kids, help them with homework, or read to them for pleasure.

• Collect clothing and household necessities to donate to a shelter or give to families who are just moving into their own homes.

• Organize food drives; go house-to-house collecting canned or dried foods.

• Hold a bake sale, car wash, or garage sale to raise money to donate to a shelter or organization that helps the homeless.

• Work with Habitat for Humanity or a similar group, donating time to help remodel housing for the homeless.

• Sponsor a drive to collect used toys and clean or repair them to distribute to homeless kids.

• Invite a homeless child to go to the library, a museum, or to the park to play.

• Help a social service organization collect unused food from large school or office cafeterias and distribute it to homeless shelters.

• Volunteer at a shelter to help serve food, register people, or just talk and be friendly with them.

• Organize a used book drive and donate the books to homeless families or shelters.

• Baby-sit for homeless families while parents are at school or work, or trying to find a job.

# Glossary

**acting out:** Misbehaving or being disruptive in the hope of calling attention to oneself.

**AFDC:** Aid to Families with Dependent Children; the federal government's primary program for helping poor and homeless children by supplying money for food, housing, and other living expenses.

**almshouse:** Eighteenth-century term for a privately financed home for the poor. Alms is help or charity given to the poor.

**barracks-style shelter:** A type of shelter for the homeless, so called because inside it looks like an army barracks. Usually barracks shelters are run by local governments in big buildings such as unused auditoriums or gymnasiums. Cots are set up where people can spend the night and get advice on where to go for food and medical care.

**boarder babies:** Those who have no homes and no one to care for them at birth, and so remain in the hospital indefinitely.

**eviction:** Being forced to move out of a rental home or building by the owner or landlord.

**failure to thrive:** The condition of a baby who does not gain weight fast enough after birth. If not treated, the child will die.

**family-style shelter:** The best type of shelter for the homeless, run by private organizations such as the Salvation Army or Red Cross. These shelters have clean, private rooms for families, and services to help people find food, housing, education, and jobs.

**foster care:** A state- or county-run program that provides homes for children whose parents cannot or do not care for them. Usually, foster children move in with approved families until permanent homes can be found.

**homeless:** Being without a permanent place to live or sleep at night.

**illiterate:** Unable to read and write, or to do so well enough to perform basic daily chores like reading a bus schedule, grocery shopping, or filling out simple forms.

**low birth weight:** Condition of a baby whose weight at birth is less than the average of five pounds; often caused by the mother's improper eating habits or lack of prenatal care during pregnancy. Can create physical or mental health problems for the child in later life.

**malnutrition:** A condition of poor health caused by improper eating habits. A lack of food, or a lack of proper vitamins and minerals in the food, can cause malnutrition, leading to severe physical and mental health problems and an increased chance of disease.

**poverty cycle:** The pattern of poverty carried on from one generation to the next, in which children of a family on welfare grow up to raise their own children on welfare, creating a cycle of dependence on the government.

**poverty line:** A point determined by the government, below which a family's income is not enough to pay for basic necessities like rent and food. Falling below the line usually makes the family eligible for government assistance programs. Currently the poverty line in America is a yearly income of approximately twenty thousand dollars for a family of four.

**runaways:** Children, usually teenagers, who have chosen to run away from home, often to escape abuse or violence.

**Section 8:** A plan for renting private homes or apartments to poor or homeless people, mostly paid by the government.

**self-esteem:** Self-respect; how you feel about yourself.

**settlement houses:** Nineteenth-century homes for the poor; the first was started by social worker Jane Addams in Chicago.

**shelter schools:** Schools for homeless children set up near shelters, where students can have a meal, take a shower, sleep, and get clean clothes in addition to learning. Most shelter schools run on very low budgets, but teachers are dedicated to helping their students in all areas of their lives.

**squatters:** Homeless people who live in abandoned buildings without permission.

**status offenders:** Older children who, because they are homeless or living on their own without adult supervision, are considered higher risks for crime even though they may have no criminal record.

**street people:** Homeless people, often single men, who live on the streets and sleep on park benches or sidewalks. Often they panhandle, or beg for money, and push their few belongings around in shopping carts.

**subsidized housing:** Apartments or houses for poor or homeless people that are built or funded largely by the government.

**sweatshop:** The term describing a small factory where people work long hours for low pay in dirty, unpleasant conditions.

**throwaways:** Children, usually teenagers, who have been forced by their parents to leave home, and so are homeless.

**welfare hotels:** Run-down hotels, usually in larger cities, that are used as shelters for the homeless. Owners receive large amounts of money from the government for allowing the homeless to live there. Crime and living conditions are extremely bad.

# Organizations
# to Contact

The yellow pages of most city phone books have headings titled HOMELESS SERVICES, SOCIAL SERVICE ORGANIZATIONS, and HUMAN SERVICES ORGANIZATIONS. Within are listed the names and numbers of shelters and other services that help homeless children. Many cities also have offices for national organizations like the Salvation Army, Volunteers of America, and Goodwill Industries. These are private organizations that provide meals, shelter, clothing, or counseling to homeless children and their families.

For listings of government agencies that help homeless children, look in the white pages under the name of the county and then under the heading HUMAN RESOURCES or SOCIAL SERVICES.

The following agencies or organizations also provide help to homeless children.

**Boys Town**
14100 Crawford Rd.
Boys Town, NY 68010
(402) 498-1300

A private organization whose goal is the care and treatment of troubled boys and girls ages nine to nineteen and families in crisis. Provides many services, including more than one hundred long-term residential homes for boys and girls. Offers assistance to kids in crisis nationwide via the Boys Town National Hotline: (800) 448-3000.

## Child Welfare League of America (CWLA)
440 First St. NW, Suite 310
Washington, DC 20001-2085
(202) 638-2952

An association of public and private agencies and organizations that serve at-risk children, youths, and their families. CWLA is involved in all areas of child welfare, from teen pregnancy to drug dependency, including foster care, group residential care of children and young adults, housing and homelessness, and family services. CWLA is the world's largest publisher of materials on child welfare.

## Covenant House
346 W. 17th St.
New York, NY 10011-5002
(212) 727-4000

An international organization helping children twelve to twenty-one years of age. Most are homeless and living on their own. Operates a mobile outreach program that provides food and counseling to children on the street. Some branches have shelters for temporary lodging. Phone counselors are available to help with physical, mental, and social problems—call the Nineline: (800) 999-9999.

## Habitat for Humanity
Habitat and Church Streets
Americus, GA 31709
(912) 924-6935

An organization of volunteers with branches throughout the United States and around the world that builds and renovates housing for low-income people.

## Homes for the Homeless
36 Cooper Square, 6th Fl.
New York, NY 10003
(212) 529-5252

Largest single provider of residential educational training services to homeless families. Works to provide homeless children and their families with education, employment training, and support services.

## Housing Assistance Council
1025 Vermont Ave. NW, #606
Washington, DC 20005
(202) 842-8600

A national nonprofit corporation that makes decent housing available for rural children from low-income families.

## Institute for Children and Poverty
36 Cooper Square, 1st Fl.
New York, NY 10003
(212) 674-2607

Works to combat the impact of homelessness and urban poverty on the lives of children and their families through development of meaningful public policy programs and by distributing research and findings pertinent to the issue. A division of Homes for the Homeless.

## Interagency Council on the Homeless
451 Seventh St. NW
Washington, DC 20410
(202) 708-1480

An agency of the federal government created as a result of the Stewart B. McKinney Homeless Assistance Act of 1987. Major activities include planning and coordinating federal actions to assist the homeless, monitoring assistance that is provided to homeless people by the government, providing technical assistance to communities that help the homeless, and providing information on federal government money and services that are available to help the homeless.

**Los Angeles Youth Network**
1550 Gower St.
Los Angeles, CA 90028
(213) 957-7364

An agency for runaway, homeless, and throwaway adolescents, ages twelve to seventeen. Provides shelter, food, and counseling.

**National Alliance to End Homelessness**
1518 K St. NW, #206
Washington, DC 20005
(202) 638-1526

A membership organization of people, companies, organizations, and government agencies dedicated to ending homelessness. Members work to provide affordable housing, find jobs that pay a living wage to workers, and offer services for the homeless. The group has several publications, including *What You Can Do to Help the Homeless*.

**National Law Center on Homelessness and Poverty**
918 F St. NW, #412
Washington, DC 20004
(202) 638-2535

A legal organization committed to finding solutions to the causes of homelessness through litigation (arguing in court on behalf of the homeless), legislation (working toward passage of laws to help the homeless), and public education about the problem.

**National Resource Center on Homelessness and Mental Illness**
c/o Policy Research Assoc.
262 Delaware Ave.
Delmar, NY 12054
(800) 444-7415

Provides information on services for mentally ill homeless people, including children and adolescents. Publishes books and resource lists; sponsors conferences, workshops, and training sessions; and conducts research.

### U.S. Department of Housing and Urban Development (HUD)
Office of Special Needs Assistance Program
451 Seventh St. SW, Room 7262
Washington, DC 20410-7000
(202) 708-4300

This division of HUD administers several programs for the homeless, including the Emergency Shelter Grants Program, Supportive Housing Program, Shelter Plus Care, and HUD-Owned Single Family Property Disposition.

### Youth Development International
5331 Mt. Alifan Dr.
San Diego, CA 92111
(619) 292-5683

Responds to the needs of young people suffering from physical, emotional, spiritual, and social problems. Offers a residential treatment center for runaways and disturbed young people. Sponsors a twenty-four-hour crisis hotline called Hit Home that serves young people in distress across the United States and Canada. Call Hit Home at (800) HIT-HOME.

# Suggestions for Further Reading

Laurie Beckleman, *The Facts About the Homeless*. New York: Macmillan, 1989.

Patricia Connors, *Runaways: Coping at Home and on the Street*. New York: Rosen, 1989.

Kevin Cwayna, *Knowing Where the Fountains Are*. Minneapolis: Deaconess Press, 1993.

Loretta Holz, *Foster Child*. New York: Julian Messner, 1984.

Thomas L. Kenyon, with Justine Blau, *What You Can Do to Help the Homeless*. New York: Simon & Schuster, 1991.

Elaine Landau, *The Homeless*. New York: Julian Messner, 1987.

Doug Marx, *The Homeless*. Vero Beach, FL: The Rourke Corporation, 1990.

Mary Rose McGeady, *God's Lost Children*. New York: Covenant House, 1991.

Teresa O'Neill, *The Homeless*. San Diego: Greenhaven Press, 1990.

Ellen Switzer, *Anyplace but Here*. New York: Atheneum, 1992.

# Works Consulted

**Books**

Jeffrey Artenstein, *Runaways: In Their Own Words*. New York: Tom Doherty Associates, 1990.

Judith Berck, *No Place to Be: Voices of Homeless Children*. New York: Houghton Mifflin, 1992.

Robert C. Coates, *A Street Is Not a Home*. Buffalo, NY: Prometheus Books, 1990.

Joan J. Johnson, *Kids Without Homes*. New York: Franklin Watts, 1991.

Anna Kosof, *Homeless in America*. New York: Franklin Watts, 1988.

Jonathan Kozol, *Rachael and Her Children*. New York: Crown, 1988.

Arnold Madison, *Runaway Teens: An American Tragedy*. New York: Elsevier/Nelson Books, 1979.

National Resource Center on Homelessness and Mental Illness, *National Organizations Concerned with Mental Health, Housing, and Homelessness*. Delmar, NY: National Resource Center, 1995.

Lisa Orr, ed., *The Homeless: Opposing Viewpoints*. San Diego: Greenhaven Press, 1990.

Robert D. Reed and Danek S. Kaus, *Runaway Children: How and Where to Find Facts and Get Help*. Saratoga, CA: R&E Publishers, 1993.

Bruce Ritter, *Covenant House: Lifeline to the Street*. New York: Doubleday, 1987.

Lois Stavsky and I. E. Mozeson, *The Place I Call Home: Faces and Voices of Homeless Teens*. New York: Shapolsky, 1990.

**Periodicals**

Claudia Glenn Dowling, "The Sins of the Fathers," *Life*, May 1995.

Colin Greer, "Something Is Robbing Our Children of Their Future," *Parade*, March 5, 1995.

Tilly Grey, "Building Communities from the Inside Out," *Habitat World*, August/September 1995.

David Handelman, "Unsettled Lives," *Vogue*, June 1994.

Jon D. Hull, "Running Scared," *Time*, November 21, 1994.

Mary Rose McGeady, "Welfare Reform: The View from Covenant House," *America*, September 24, 1994.

Claudia Pearce, "Looking for a Place to Call Home," *On Air*, October 1994.

William Plummer and Cathy Free, "Shelter in the Heart," *People*, November 7, 1994.

"When You Wish upon a Star," *Teen*, November 1993.

# Index

# About the Author

Eleanor H. Ayer is the author of more than two dozen books for children and young adults, several of which deal with social issues. Among them are *Teen Fatherhood*, *Teen Marriage*, *Teen Suicide*, *Stress*, and *Depression*. She has also written several biographies and books dealing with World War II and the Holocaust.

Mrs. Ayer has a master's degree in literacy journalism from Syracuse University's Newhouse School of Journalism. The mother of two boys, she lives in Frederick, Colorado, where she and her husband operate a small book publishing company.

# Picture Credits